Whose House?

Colin & Jacqui Hawkins

Collins

An Imprint of HarperCollins*Publishers*

Whose house is this
with its cosy thatch?

Who left the door upon the latch?

Who ate the porridge and broke the chair?

And slept in the bed of the littlest bear?

Along the winding lane and over the wooden stile…

Whose house is this
so trim and neat?

Who lives here with great big feet?

Who's hairy, scary and very tough?

But can he frighten the Billy Goats Gruff?

Over the wooden stile and across the rickety bridge…

Whose house is this
so grand and tall?
Whose ugly sisters are off to the ball?
Who's left behind to scrub the floors,
wash the dishes and do the chores?

Across the rickety bridge, through the town and up Royal Hill…

Whose palace is this
with its towers and flags?
Who's the fine lady no longer in rags?
Who are the guests having fun at the ball?
Look inside and you'll see them all
—well, nearly all.